HARDWOOD GREATS
PRO BASKETBALL'S BEST PLAYERS

JAMES HARDEN

HARDWOOD GREATS
PRO BASKETBALL'S BEST PLAYERS

CHRIS PAUL

GIANNIS ANTETOKOUNMPO

JAMES HARDEN

KEVIN DURANT

LEBRON JAMES

PAUL GEORGE

RUSSELL WESTBROOK

STEPHEN CURRY

HARDWOOD GREATS

PRO BASKETBALL'S BEST PLAYERS

JAMES HARDEN

DONALD PARKER

MASON CREST

PHILADELPHIA

MIAMI

Mason Crest
450 Parkway Drive, Suite D
Broomall, Pennsylvania 19008
(866) MCP-BOOK (toll-free)
www.masoncrest.com

First printing
9 8 7 6 5 4 3 2 1

ISBN (hardback) 978-1-4222-4347-3
ISBN (series) 978-1-4222-4344-2
ISBN (ebook) 978-1-4222-7462-0

Cataloging-in-Publication Data on file with the Library of Congress

Developed and Produced by National Highlights Inc.
Editor: Andrew Luke
Interior and cover design: Annalisa Gumbrecht, Studio Gumbrecht
Production: Michelle Luke

QR CODES AND LINKS TO THIRD-PARTY CONTENT

CONTENTS

KEY ICONS TO LOOK FOR:

 Words to Understand: These words with their easy-to-understand definitions will increase the reader's understanding of the text while building vocabulary skills.

 Sidebars: This boxed material within the main text allows readers to build knowledge, gain insights, explore possibilities, and broaden their perspectives by weaving together additional information to provide realistic and holistic perspectives.

 Educational Videos: Readers can view videos by scanning our QR codes, providing them with additional educational content to supplement the text. Examples include news coverage, moments in history, speeches, iconic sports moments, and much more!

 Text-Dependent Questions: These questions send the reader back to the text for more careful attention to the evidence presented there.

 Research Projects: Readers are pointed toward areas of further inquiry connected to each chapter. Suggestions are provided for projects that encourage deeper research and analysis.

 Series Glossary of Key Terms: This back-of-the-book glossary contains terminology used throughout this series. Words found here increase the reader's ability to read and comprehend higher-level books and articles in this field.

WORDS TO UNDERSTAND

adorn: To decorate or add beauty to

deficit: A reduction in value; a lack or shortage

phenomenal: Highly extraordinary or prodigious

versatile: Having or capable of many uses

CHAPTER 1

GREATEST MOMENTS

THE NBA CAREER OF JAMES HARDEN

James Edward Harden, Jr., known as The Beard (in recognition of the long black beard that **adorns** his face), has become one of the best-scoring guards in NBA history. Since being drafted third overall in the 2009 NBA draft as the first-ever draft choice of the newly formed Oklahoma City Thunder, Harden has led the league in several categories, including scoring during the 2017-2018 and 2018-2019 seasons, free throws made for five consecutive seasons (2014–2015 to 2018–2019), and free throws attempted for six seasons (2012–2013; 2014–2015 to 2018–2019). He has risen to become one of the most feared scorers in the NBA, and after winning his first MVP award in 2017, the sky is the limit as to how much more we will see from him.

Harden has firmly established himself as one of the premier guards in the NBA.

Harden always saw himself as an NBA player, carrying a basketball with him everywhere he went as a child. He wasn't, however, the most disciplined person when he was younger and developing his game. He didn't like practicing and wasn't in the shape that he is in today. But he had a desire to make it to the NBA. Influenced by a high school coach who saw his potential and encouraged by a single mother (who worked hard to support him), an older brother, and an older sister, Harden changed his habits, put in the effort, and made it to a big-time college program at Arizona State and then to the NBA.

Harden has worked hard to establish himself as one of the premier guards in the league. At 6 feet 5 inches (1.96 m) and 220 pounds (99.79 kg), he has become **versatile** enough to excel at both the shooting guard and point guard positions on the court. This versatility has earned him the respect of other players in the league and a few national television commercials and put him on track to join the greatest guards the league has seen as a member of the Basketball Hall of Fame located in Springfield, Massachusetts. He has already been named to several all-star teams, was a member of the all-rookie team after his first year in the league in 2009, and as chosen to represent the United States in the 2012 Summer Olympics.

Harden has exceeded expectations and has succeeded in a league where success can be hard to come by. He has become an all-around scorer and also gets other players involved in the game. Harden has played on two successful teams in Oklahoma City and Houston and has been honored with awards, has been selected for all-star teams, and has played for the US Men's National Basketball team. He has recorded many great moments in his NBA career and has many more ahead of him as he continues to play.

HARDEN'S GREATEST CAREER MOMENTS

HERE IS A LIST OF

SOME OF THE CAREER

FIRSTS AND GREATEST

ACHIEVEMENTS DURING

HIS TIME IN THE NBA:

Harden started his NBA career in Oklahoma City as a bench player with the Thunder.

FIRST CAREER TRIPLE-DOUBLE

In a February 2, 2013, home game against the Charlotte Bobcats, Harden completed his first career triple-double. He contributed 21 points, 11 assists, and 11 rebounds for the game and was one of three Rockets players with 20 points or more in the game. His effort was instrumental in helping the Rockets to a 109–95 victory over the Bobcats.

Video highlights of James Harden leading the Houston Rockets in a 109–95 home win against the Charlotte Bobcats, where he recorded his first career triple-double, February 2, 2013.

FIRST NBA ALL-STAR GAME APPEARANCE

Harden was selected as a representative of the Western Conference squad in his first all-star game appearance on February 17, 2013. The game was played in Houston, featuring potential Hall of Fame members Kobe Bryant, Tim Duncan, Kevin Durant, Kevin Garnett, LeBron James, Tony Parker, Chris Paul, and Dwyane Wade. Coming off the bench, Harden contributed 15 points in 25 minutes of action as the West All-Stars beat the East, 143–138.

Watch a recap of James Harden's 15-point effort in his first-ever NBA All-Star game appearance as a member of the Houston Rockets, playing in his hometown. Harden helped the West defeat the East, 143–138.

NAMED NBA MOST VALUABLE PLAYER (2017–2018)

It had been ten years since a shooting guard was the recipient of the league's MVP award (LA Laker star Kobe Bryant won in 2008), that is, until the end of the 2017–2018 season when Harden won his first MVP trophy. Harden averaged 30.4 points a game and scored 2,191 points, 8.6 assists per game (620 for the season), 3.7 three-pointers a game (265 total in 2017–2018), and sported a field goal percentage of 44.9.

Check out this NBA "mix-tape" featuring highlights from Harden's 2017–2018 MVP season.

NBA SCORING CHAMPION (2017–2018)

The 2017–2018 season was a **phenomenal** season for Harden. Not only did he win his first MVP award as the league's top player, he also earned his first award as the league's top scorer. His 2,171 points and 30.4 points per game (ppg) average led all scorers for the season, including Anthony Davis (New Orleans Pelicans, 28.1 ppg), LeBron James (Cleveland Cavaliers, now Los Angeles Lakers, 27.5 ppg), Damian Lillard (Portland Trailblazers, 26.9 ppg), and Giannis Antetokounmpo (Milwaukee Bucks, 26.9 ppg).

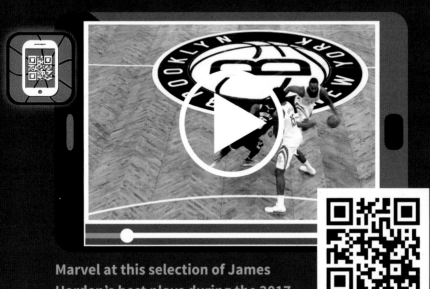

Marvel at this selection of James Harden's best plays during the 2017–2018 season, which led to his winning the league's scoring championship.

5

REACHED 10,000 CAREER POINTS

Harden scored 30 points and 15 assists, turning in a double-double against the New York Knicks. The Houston Rockets won the game 118–99, and the 30-point effort put Harden over the 10,000 points scored mark for his career in the NBA.

Highlights of James Harden's 30-point, 15-assist, 6-rebound performance on November 2, 2016, against the New York Knicks in a 118–99 road victory. His performance helped Harden reach the 10,000-point career milestone.

FIRST PLAYER IN NBA HISTORY TO SCORE A 60-POINT TRIPLE-DOUBLE IN A GAME

Harden made NBA history in a home game against the Orlando Magic on January 30, 2018. He made 19 of 30 field goals for a spectacular 63.3 percent shooting and 60 total points. This production went along with 10 total rebounds and 11 assists, as the Rockets defeated the Magic 114–107. Harden became the first player to record a 60-point triple-double.

Highlights of James Harden's history-making performance against the Orlando Magic for the league's first 60-point triple-double, January 30, 2018.

NAMED NBA SIXTH MAN OF THE YEAR (2011–2012)

Harden began his career as a member of the Oklahoma City Thunder (as their first-ever draft pick once the team moved from Seattle). In his third (and final) year with the Thunder, a team that featured future MVPs Russell Westbrook and Kevin Durant (now with Golden State Warriors), Harden found playing time as a sixth man, or first bench player called into a game. His role in 62 games played (two of which he started) helped lead the Thunder to an overall 47–19 win-loss record and a Western Conference Championship. His performance that season also earned Harden the NBA Sixth Man of the Year award.

The top ten plays of James Harden's 2011–2012 NBA season as a member of the Oklahoma City Thunder.

SCORED 45 POINTS IN WESTERN CONFERENCE FINALS AGAINST GOLDEN STATE WARRIORS, MAY 25, 2015

Harden, in his first Western Conference Finals appearance, did everything he could as a team leader to rally his Houston Rockets team back into the series against the reigning NBA champion Golden State Warriors. Harden's Rockets faced a three-games-to-none **deficit** and possible elimination from the series, but won 128–115 thanks to Harden's effort to prolong the series.

Highlights of James Harden's 45-point effort against the Golden State Warriors in Game 4 of the 2014–2015 Western Conference Finals, May 25, 2015.

Harden goes in for a layup in a 2016 game against Washington.

TEXT-DEPENDENT QUESTIONS

1. Which team selected James Harden with the third overall pick in the 2009 NBA draft?

2. In what statistical categories did he lead the league in the 2017–2018 NBA season?

3. What NBA players (past and present), besides Harden, led the league in free throws made for four consecutive years or more?

RESEARCH PROJECT

The free throw can be one of the most difficult shots to hit consistently in a basketball game. One of the reasons is because a player stands alone, one-on-one with the basket, while an arena full of fans attempt to distract or unnerve the shooter enough to lose focus and concentration. He has proven to be one of the most consistent free throw shooters in the history of the NBA.

Find out when the free throw shot was first introduced to the game of basketball. Determine what distance a free throw shooter must stand from the basket when attempting this type of shot and which player in NBA history made the most free throws in a single game.

WORDS TO UNDERSTAND

accolades: Any award, honor, or notice containing or expressing praise

athleticism: The physical qualities that are characteristic of athletes, such as strength, fitness, and agility

notorious: Widely and unfavorably known

CHAPTER 2

THE ROAD TO THE TOP

There's no changing the fact that Harden has the skills that make him one of the best guards in the NBA. How do his skills stack up to those of some of the greatest players to ever play the position? Here is a look at the stats for players at the same performance level as Harden through their first nine years in the NBA. The list includes Jerry West, former Houston Rockets great Clyde Drexler, Walt Frazier, and Reggie Miller:

PLAYER	PTS	PPG	FG	FGA	3PT	3PTA	FT	FTA
Jerry West*	16835	27.51	5933	12658	0	0	4969	6133
James Harden	*15809*	*23.01*	*4656*	*10502*	*1647*	*4523*	*4850*	*5678*
Dwyane Wade	14990	25.15	5292	10899	324	1113	4082	5301
Clyde Drexler*	14857	20.95	5761	11792	275	939	3060	3908
Stephen Curry	14434	23.09	5017	10509	2129	4880	2271	2514
Reggie Miller*	14073	19.55	4627	9423	1203	3032	3616	4122
Walt Frazier*	13294	19.46	5204	10580	0	0	2886	3681
Magic Johnson*	12213	19.11	4483	8406	58	302	3189	3876
Chris Paul	11496	18.63	4036	8545	612	1712	2812	3280
John Stockton*	10870	13.32	3883	7578	359	1019	2745	3340

Members of Basketball Hall of Fame.

Fourteen-time All-Star and NBA Hall of Fame legend Jerry West, now a successful executive in the NBA, is the caliber of player whose stats compare to those that Harden put up in the first nine seasons of his career.

Harden's numbers for the first nine years of his career are similar to current and future Hall of Famers, including the player whose image is the current NBA logo (Jerry West). For this time frame, his total points scored (15,809), three-point shots made (1,647), and three-point shots attempted (4,523) all rank second when compared to arguably the ten best guards that have ever played basketball in the NBA. Harden certainly has the chance to go past the career totals of these and other legends of the game.

Harden has been able to keep pace with class standout and two-time NBA MVP (and three-time NBA Champion) Stephen Curry of the Golden State Warriors. Their ability to direct their respective teams on the court and take on different roles has made them feared by competitors. Both are comfortable with scoring, assisting, and getting teammates involved and have a desire to win, not just their regular season games but in the playoffs as well.

Like Stephen Curry, Harden is also an NBA MVP. Curry, however, unlike Harden, has multiple NBA championships.

NBA DRAFT DAY 2009 SIGNIFICANT ACCOUNTS

- James Harden was selected by Oklahoma City (Thunder) with the third pick in the first round of the 2009 NBA draft.

- He was the first-ever draft selection of the Oklahoma City Thunder, who had moved from Seattle as the former Seattle Supersonics.

- Harden was one of eight players from the Pac-10 (now Pac-12) drafted.

- The 2009 NBA draft was held at Madison Square Garden located in New York City on June 25, 2009.

- The 2009 NBA draft was the first to

feature three sons of former NBA players: Stephen Curry, drafted seventh by the Golden State Warriors (Dell Curry); Gerald Henderson, Jr., drafted twelfth by the Charlotte Bobcats (Gerald Henderson Sr.), and, Austin Daye who was drafted fifteenth by the Detroit Pistons (Darren Daye).

- Blake Griffin, the overall number-one draft selection, was picked by the Los Angeles Clippers. Griffin missed the 2009–2010 season due to injury; Tyreke Evans, the fourth overall pick by the Sacramento Kings, was named the 2009–2010 Rookie of the Year. Griffin played in the 2010–2011 NBA season and won Rookie of the Year honors, becoming the first two players taken in the same NBA draft to win back-to-back Rookie of the Year honors.

- Harden was the first guard drafted in the 2009 NBA draft.

- He was one of 31 guards taken in the 2009 NBA draft out of the sixty players drafted in rounds 1 and 2.

- Of the 31 guards selected, only 15 are still active in the NBA (2017–2018). A total of 19 players are still active as of the 2017–2018 season, making the guard position the largest representative group from the 2009 NBA draft.

ATHLETIC ACCOMPLISHMENTS IN HIGH SCHOOL AND COLLEGE

Harden was born on August 26, 1989, in Los Angeles, California, to James Harden, Sr., and Monja Willis. Harden's mother worked in customer service with AT&T for thirty years while father James, Sr., was a veteran of the US Navy. Harden is the youngest of three children.

Harden grew up in the **notorious** Compton section of Los Angeles with his mother and two older siblings, a sister by the name of Arnique Jelks (born in 1980) and brother Akili Roberson (born in 1976). Sports became a way for him and his siblings to stay away from gangs and focus on becoming strong, independent adults.

While his brother Akili Roberson excelled in football, James focused his talent on basketball. His brother, in fact, was a highly regarded two-way player, as a starting quarterback on offense and a defensive back while attending Alain Leroy Locke High School in Los Angeles. He earned All-City Honors and played at LA Southwest Community College before moving to Kansas University in Lawrence, Kansas, to play one year (1997) as a backup quarterback for the Jayhawks football team. After college, he also spent time in the National Indoor Football League, playing quarterback for the Staten Island (NY) Xtreme in 2004.

HIGH SCHOOL

While his brother was earning **accolades** on the football field, James focused on becoming a professional basketball player. Harden's brother is quoted saying about his younger brother, "He carried around a basketball as if it was his job. I was like, 'Dude, do you know how many people play in the NBA?'" Knowing how many people actually made it to the NBA did not keep Harden from setting his sights on making it big time and becoming one of the league's premier players.

Harden's mother also noted that he didn't start out dedicated to preparing his body physically in order to meet the demands of an NBA player. He always knew that he wanted to become one of the best basketball players in the world, but Willis commented, "When it was time to run around the gym and do sit-ups, he wasn't trying to do all that."

Harden grew up in Compton, a section of the Los Angeles area known for its high crime rate.

Harden enrolled at Artesia High School (nicknamed the "Bulldogs") in neighboring Lakewood, California, in 2004. Known as a Los Angeles–area powerhouse in high school basketball, his coach Scott Pera began molding him into the player he would later become in the NBA. Although Harden complained about the physical training , the bond that developed between him and coach Pera paid off as he earned status as a high school All-American in his senior year.

Harden became a top high school prospect in the country and a recruiting target of coach Roy Williams at the University of North Carolina, one of the top programs in the NCAA. Instead, Harden chose to stay close to home and play in nearby Tempe, Arizona, for the Arizona State University Sun Devils and coach Herb Sendek. Harden's high school coach was a one-time assistant at Arizona State, which, in part, influenced his decision to attend the school and play for the program.

COLLEGE

Arizona State University had just come off an 8–22 win/loss season the year prior to Harden joining the squad as a freshman for the 2007–2008 school year. The decision to join the Sun Devils squad paid off immediately. The team improved in Harden's first year by thirteen wins to finish 21–12 in a sixth-place finish in the Pac-10 Conference.

This finish resulted in Arizona State earning a number-one seed in the National Invitational Tournament, where they reached the quarterfinals.

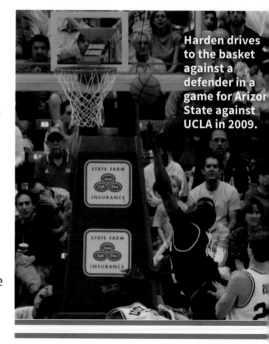

Harden drives to the basket against a defender in a game for Arizona State against UCLA in 2009.

Harden led the Sun Devils in his second year to an identical 21–12 record and a third place Pac-10 (now Pac-12) Conference finish. The team was invited to play in the NCAA Men's Basketball tournament in 2009, where they made it to the tournament's second round.

His career totals during his time at Arizona State University (two years) are:

Year	PTS	PPG	FG	FGA	3PT	3PTA	FT	FTA
2007–2008	605	17.8	196	372	44	108	169	224
2008–2009	704	20.1	221	452	58	163	204	270
TOTALS	**1309**	**19.0**	**417**	**824**	**102**	**271**	**373**	**494**

Harden chose to leave the Sun Devils after his sophomore year and focus on establishing himself in the NBA. His efforts during the 2008–2009 season led to his being named Pac-10 Player of the Year. Harden was also named as a consensus first team All-American, along with Blake Griffin (Oklahoma University), DeJuan Blair (University of Pittsburgh), Stephen Curry (Davidson University), and Tyler Hansbrough (University of North Carolina). Harden was also a finalist for the John R. Wooden Award. The Wooden Award, created in 1976, is given each year to college basketball's outstanding player. The award is named after the legendary UCLA coach, John R. Wooden.

Blake Griffin of Oklahoma was the winner of the 2009 John R. Wooden Award as college basketball's Player of the Year. Harden finished seventh in the voting.

NBA DRAFT DAY 2009

Harden decided to leave college and declare early for the 2009 NBA draft. He participated in the 2009 NBA Pre-Draft Combine (located in Chicago), where he displayed his athleticism by posting the following results:

- Measurements (height, weight): 6 feet 5 inches (1.86 m), 222 pounds (99.79 kg)

- No-step vertical jump: 31.5 inches (0.80 m)

- Maximum vertical jump: 37.0 inches (0.94 m)

- No-step vertical jump height: 11 feet 3 inches (3.43 m)

- Maximum vertical jump height: 11 feet 8.5 inches (3.57 m)

- Bench press (185 pounds–repetitions): 17

- Lane agility: 11.1 seconds

- Three-quarter-court sprint: 3.13 seconds

If teams could take a time machine back to the 2009 draft knowing what we know today, the draft would likely go quite differently. For example, two-time NBA MVP Stephen Curry would likely not be the third point guard to be drafted. The most significant change would likely occur with the second pick. Five-time NBA All-Star Blake Griffin was the first pick by the LA Clippers, and he has had a very good career. At number two, however, Memphis selected University of Connecticut center Hasheem Thabeet. Thabeet started a total of only twenty NBA games in his short five-season NBA career. James Harden—the 2017 MVP—was the third pick of the draft. Oh, what might have been for the Grizzlies, who went to the Western Conference Finals in 2013, had Harden been in the fold.

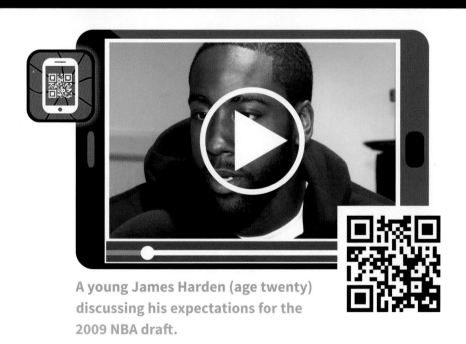

A young James Harden (age twenty) discussing his expectations for the 2009 NBA draft.

Hasheem Thabeet (34) was the second player taken in the NBA draft, one spot ahead of Harden.

HARDEN AND THE 2009 NBA DRAFT CLASS

The 2009 NBA draft took place on June 25, 2009, and was held in New York City. A total of sixty players were selected in the draft's two rounds; fifty of the sixty chosen played at least one game in the NBA. As of the 2017–2018 season, nineteen players drafted in 2009 still played in the NBA.

Harden was selected by the Oklahoma City Thunder with the third overall pick in the 2009 NBA draft. The selection was the first for Oklahoma City, which had moved the season prior from Seattle (where they played as the Seattle Supersonics). The Minnesota Timberwolves had the most selections in the draft with six (four first-round picks and two second-round selections), followed by the Portland Trailblazers with four (one first-round selection and three second-round selections). All of Minnesota's first-round picks were guards, but none were any of the six NBA All-Star guards taken. The two NBA teams that did not make a selection in the 2009 draft were the Houston Rockets and Orlando Magic.

There were a total of 31 guards selected in the draft, which represents 52 percent of all of the players drafted in rounds one and two in 2009. Eight centers were drafted, representing 13 percent of all players drafted and the lowest of the three positions selected. Twelve of the players selected in the 2009 draft came from Europe or Africa.

Here are the important statistics of the top-ten active players in the NBA from the 2009 draft, ranked in order of total points scored (through the 2017–2018 season):

Draft#	Player	Team	POS	G	PTS	AST	STL	3PT	FG	FT
3	James Harden	OKC Thunder	PG/SG	765	18,627	4,743	1,189	2,025	5,499	5,604
7	Stephen Curry	Golden State Warriors	PG	694	16,315	4,588	1,200	2,483	5,649	2,534
9	DeMar DeRozan	Toronto Raptors	SG	752	14,931	2,553	741	332	5,347	3,905
1	Blake Griffin	LA Clippers	PF	604	13,200	2,690	547	380	4,961	2,898
17	Jrue Holiday	Philadelphia 76ers	PG/SG	652	10,148	4,151	964	805	4,009	1,325
4	Tyreke Evans	Sacramento Kings	PG/SG/SF	594	9,347	2,852	734	500	3,510	1,827
19	Jeff Teague	Atlanta Hawks	PG	712	9,049	4,145	858	629	3,212	1,996
21	Darren Collison	New Orleans Hornets	PG	708	8.857	3,543	819	635	3,270	1,682
26	Taj Gibson	Chicago Bulls	PF	737	7,239	760	423	22	2,999	1,219

Harden was drafted four selections ahead of Stephen Curry out of Davidson University. Curry was selected by the Golden State Warriors with the seventh pick overall. Tyreke Evans was the second guard drafted in the 2009 NBA draft, selected number four overall by the Sacramento Kings. Evans went on to be named the Rookie of the Year for the 2009–2010 season.

The Minnesota Timberwolves, with picks five and six, chose point guards Ricky Rubio (the first player born in the 1990s drafted in the NBA) of the Euroleague and Jonny Flynn of Syracuse University. The Timberwolves also spent their eighteenth pick in the first round on University of North Carolina

DeMar DeRozan was the ninth player and third shooting guard selected in the 2009 NBA draft.

Minnesota used the first of its four first-round picks to select Spanish guard Ricky Rubio at the 2009 NBA draft.

point guard Ty Lawson, who was traded to the Denver Nuggets, and shooting guard Wayne Ellington, also from the University of North Carolina. This made a total of four guards drafted by Minnesota in the 2009 NBA draft. Only Rubio and Lawson were active players (with different teams) as of the 2017–2018 NBA season.

TEXT-DEPENDENT QUESTIONS

1. What honors and awards did Harden receive in his second year at Arizona State University (2008–2009)?

2. How many total players were selected in the 2009 NBA draft? How many guards were selected? How many centers were selected?

3. Which NBA team(s) did not select players in the 2009 NBA draft?

RESEARCH PROJECT

Guards are the players responsible for controlling and distributing the basketball, as well as providing offense. Considered the team's "playmaker," the position has a lot of similarities to that of the quarterback in football.

Harden plays both guard positions, running the point and directing the offense and making shots as the number two or shooting guard. He is able to hit shots from both outside and inside the three-point line and is one of the more consistent free throw shooters in the NBA.

List your choices for the top five shooting guards and the top five point guards in NBA history. Determine what statistics you want to use to choose which players make your rankings, which could be total points scored, or three-point shots made (keep in mind that the three-point shot made its NBA debut in 1979), and use the same ones to create your two top-five lists.

WORDS TO UNDERSTAND

formidable: Causing fear, apprehension, or dread

showcase: Prominently or proudly regarded or presented

triumvirate: Any group of three people associated in some way

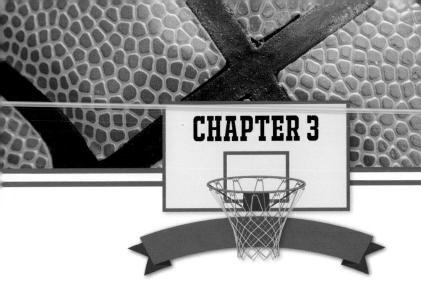

CHAPTER 3

ON THE COURT

As a player in the NBA (nine-year career from 2009 through the 2017–2018 season), he was named league MVP, 2017–2018. He was runner-up in the MVP voting in 2016–2017 to his former Oklahoma City Thunder teammate Russell Westbrook. He had 15,809 total points scored, ranking him first among all of the 2009 draft choices, including Stephen Curry (who is second with 14,434 total points through 2018).

Harden has made 4,850 free throws on 5,678 attempts, first among all 2009 draft choices. He has also made 4,656 field goals on 10,502 field-goal attempts (second among all 2009 draft choices behind Stephen Curry of Golden State Warriors) and has appeared in the Western Conference Finals four times, in 2011 and 2012, as a member of the Oklahoma City Thunder and in 2015 and 2018 as a member of the Houston Rockets. Harden has made an appearance in the NBA Finals one time in his career in 2012 while playing for Oklahoma City against the LeBron James–led Miami Heat (who won the championship).

Harden faced his former team, Oklahoma City, in the first round of the 2013 NBA playoffs.

THE BEST IN THE NBA

Harden has been honored by the league as the best sixth man, winning the award in 2012 as a member of the Oklahoma City Thunder. Joining the Houston Rockets has allowed Harden to **showcase** his talents and come out from the shadows of his former Oklahoma City Thunder teammates, Russell Westbrook and Kevin Durant. His starring role with the Rockets has helped the team regain its position as one of the best teams in the NBA's Western Conference. It also helped Harden become recognized as not only one of the best role players in the league but as the league's Most Valuable Player for the 2017–2018 season.

JAMES HARDEN

POINT GUARD / SHOOTING GUARD

- Date of birth: August 26, 1989

- Height: 6 feet 5 inches (1.96 m); Weight: Approximately 220 pounds (99.79 kg)

- Drafted in the first round in 2009 (third pick overall) by the Oklahoma City Thunder

- College: Arizona State University

- NBA Most Valuable Player (2017-2018)

- Two-time NBA scoring leader (2017-2018, 2018-2019)

- NBA assists leader (2017)

- NBA Sixth Man of the Year (2012)

- Five-time All-NBA First Team (2014-2019)

- Named to 7 NBA All-Star teams (2013–2019)

NBA Commissioner Adam Silver announces James Harden, seen standing with his mother, Monja Willis, the winner of the KIA Motors 2017–2018 NBA Most Valuable Player.

CAREER COMPARISONS

COMPARISON WITH THE MEMBERS OF THE 2009 NBA DRAFT CLASS

Harden is one of the more productive members of the 2009 draft class. He has scored more total points (18,627) than draft picks one and two combined (Blake Griffin, who has 13,200 total points through eight seasons, and Hasheem Thabeet, a center drafted by the Memphis Grizzlies, who played in Japan in 2017–2018 and has 483 NBA career points). He has also scored more points than 2009 Rookie of the Year Tyreke Evans (9,347 points, drafted by the Sacramento Kings), Stephen Curry (16,315 with the Golden State Warriors),

DeMar DeRozan (14,931, drafted by the Toronto Raptors), and Jeff Teague (the Atlanta Hawks draft pick who has 9,049 career points through nine seasons).

Harden has 4,000 career rebounds, which ranks him third among the 2009 class behind Blake Griffin (5,417 rebounds) and Taj Gibson (4,731 rebounds). DeMar DeRozan (3,201 rebounds) and Stephen Curry (3,132 rebounds) are ranked four and five. Harden far and away is the best free throw shooter selected in the 2009 draft. His 5,604 free throws made (on 6,536 attempts) also ranks first over the next four class members: DeMar DeRozan (3,905 free throws made), Stephen Curry (2,534 free throws made), Jeff Teague (1,996 free throws made), and Tyreke Evans (1,827 free throws made).

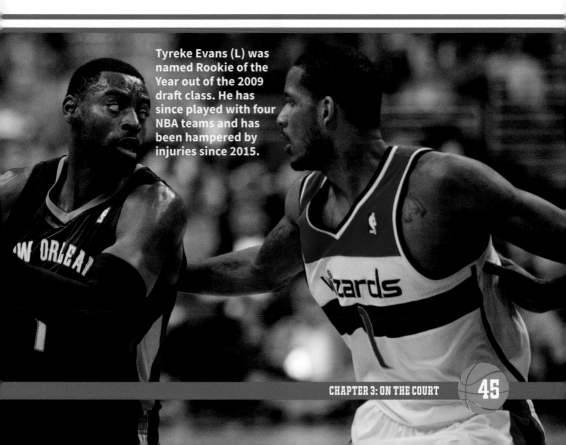

Tyreke Evans (L) was named Rookie of the Year out of the 2009 draft class. He has since played with four NBA teams and has been hampered by injuries since 2015.

Other categories that Harden ranks high in among the draftees from 2009 include three-point shots made, three-point shots attempted, field goals made, field goals attempted, steals, and assists:

THREE PT FG MADE

Stephen Curry
(Golden State Warriors)

2,483

James Harden
(Oklahoma City Thunder)

2,025

Danny Green
(Cleveland Cavaliers)

1,163

Wayne Ellington
(Minnesota Timberwolves)

966

Brandon Jennings
(Milwaukee Bucks)

914

Of the 2009 draft class, only Curry has scored more three-point field goals than Harden.

THREE PT FG ATTEMPTED

Stephen Curry
(Golden State Warriors)

5,690

James Harden
(Oklahoma City Thunder)

5,551

Daniel "Danny" Green
(Cleveland Cavaliers)

2,878

Brandon Jennings
(Milwaukee Bucks)

2,648

Wayne Ellington
(Minnesota Timberwolves)

2,546

FIELD GOALS MADE

Stephen Curry
(Golden State Warriors)

5,649

James Harden
(Oklahoma City Thunder)

5,499

DeMar DeRozan
(Toronto Raptors)

5,347

Jrue Holiday
(Philadelphia 76ers)

4,009

Tyreke Evans
(Sacramento Kings)

3,510

FIELD GOALS ATTEMPTED

James Harden
(Oklahoma City Thunder)

12,411

Stephen Curry
(Golden State Warriors)

11,849

DeMar DeRozan
(Toronto Raptors)

11,845

Jrue Holiday
(Philadelphia 76ers)

8,860

Tyreke Evans
(Sacramento Kings)

7,318

STEALS

Stephen Curry
(Golden State Warriors)

1,200

James Harden
(Oklahoma City Thunder)

1,189

Jrue Holiday
(Philadelphia 76ers)

964

Ricky Rubio
(Minnesota Timberwolves)

959

Jeff Teague
(Atlanta Hawks)

858

ASSISTS

James Harden
(Oklahoma City Thunder)

4,743

Stephen Curry
(Golden State Warriors)

4,588

Jrue Holiday
(Philadelphia 76ers)

4,151

Jeff Teague
(Atlanta Hawks)

4,145

Ricky Rubio
(Minnesota Timberwolves)

3,817

COMPARISON TO STEPHEN CURRY

James Harden and Stephen Curry were both drafted in 2009. Curry, who has spent his entire career as a member of the Golden State Warriors, has put up statistics that are almost identical to Harden's. The two men are either at the top or near the top (within the top three) of every NBA shooting category (points, free throws, field goals) as well as ball handling and defensive categories (assists, steals, rebounds).

Both players made the All-Rookie team after their first season in the league. They have also both been named MVP of the league and have collected other individual honors, placing Harden and Curry at the top of the class of the sixty players taken in the 2009 NBA draft. Curry has three championship rings, (including back-to-back NBA titles earned in 2017 and 2018) and was

Harden trails only Curry in terms of total field goals and steals from the 2009 draft class.

a member of the Golden State Warriors squad who broke the NBA record for most team wins in a season (73; Harden's Houston Rockets team that went 65–17 in 2017–2018 ranks twenty-first all-time on the most wins in a season list). Many experts believe it is a matter of time before Harden's Houston team starts to win its own NBA Championships.

U.S. NATIONAL TEAM

Harden with Team USA in 2012.

One of the greatest honors that Harden has earned as a result of his play on the court was being named a member of the 2012 US Men's National Basketball Team. Harden joined fellow Oklahoma City Thunder teammates Russell Westbrook and Kevin Durant, along with centers Tyson Chandler, Kevin Love, and Anthony Davis; forwards LeBron James, Andre Iguodala, and Carmelo Anthony; and guards Deron Williams, Kobe Bryant, and Chris Paul as members of the team.

The team, coached by Duke University head coach Mike Krzyzewski, represented the United States in the 2012 Summer Olympic Games in London. Following up on their 2008 Olympic gold medal and 2010 FIBA World Championship, Harden and his teammates swept through the competition to the gold medal game. Facing the **formidable** men's national team from Spain (featuring former NBA Rookie of the Year and San Antonio Spur, Paul Gasol), the United States won by the score of 107–100.

JAMES HARDEN, KEVIN DURANT, AND RUSSELL WESTBROOK

When he joined the Oklahoma City Thunder for the 2009–2010 NBA season, the team had just completed its first season away from its original home—Seattle, Washington (as the Seattle Supersonics). The team, at that time, featured future MVPs Kevin Durant (now with the Golden State Warriors) and Russell Westbrook. Harden became part of one of the league's best shooting **triumvirates** when he became a member of the Thunder.

Just how great was this formidable group of players, all assembled on the same team? Just looking at their awards, recognitions, and honors is awe-inspiring:

PLAYER	ALL-STARS GAMES	ALL-NBA HONORS	ALL-ROOKIE (Y/N)	ROY	MVP AWARD
James Harden	7	6	Y	0	1
Russell Westbrook	8	8	Y	0	1
Kevin Durant	10	9	Y	1	1
	25	23		1	3

These three players have appeared in a total of 22 NBA All-Star games, been named to twenty All-NBA squads and All-Rookie teams, and have each won the league's MVP award.

TEXT-DEPENDENT QUESTIONS

1. What year did Harden win the NBA's Most Valuable Player (MVP) award?

2. How many players were selected in the 2009 NBA draft ahead of him?

3. What other future MVPs did Harden play with during his first three years in the NBA (as a member of the Oklahoma City Thunder)?

RESEARCH PROJECT

The trio of James Harden, Russell Westbrook, and Kevin Durant was one of the most exciting and fun group of players to watch play on the same team. There are several such groups of three players in NBA history who have helped each other and their teams consistently make the playoffs and win NBA championships. Find and list three such groups of three players, the team they played for, the seasons (years) they played together, and the number of honors, awards, and championships (both conference and league) they won together.

 WORDS TO UNDERSTAND

burden : Duty; responsibility

franchise: A team and its operating organization having the right of membership in a professional sports league

subordinate: Occupying a lower class, rank, or position

CHAPTER 4

WORDS COUNT

When the time comes to address the media before or after a game, players either retreat to the comfort of traditional phrases that avoid controversy (Cliché City), or they speak their mind with refreshing candor (Quote Machine).

Here are ten quotes, compiled in part from the website 247Sports.com, which lend some insight into the personality of James Harden.

"I heard a lot of those things. I heard that I was greedy; that I didn't care about winning; heard the questioning of my loyalty. And I'm thinking: 'Of course I want to win. I've been winning my entire life.'"

One of the criticisms that Harden has received over the years regarding his game and style of play is that he does not like to share the ball or that he cares more about his personal statistics and not winning. However, the numbers since joining the Houston Rockets tell a different story.

After Harden joined the Rockets, Houston's average win total increased by 20 percent over what it had been for the prior ten years.

For the decade of the 2000s, prior to his joining the Rockets (2000–2012), the team averaged 44 wins and 37 losses. The highest win season was 55 in 2007–2008, and the team went as far as the Western Conference semifinals in the 2008–2009 NBA season. When Harden became a Rocket in the 2012–2013 season, the average win total rose by nine to 53 and losses decreased to an average of 29 per season.

During Harden's MVP season of 2017–2018, the Rockets posted a record of 65 wins and 17 losses, the best record in the league and the best win/loss record the Rockets have had in their fifty-one–year **franchise** history. Harden was fourth in the NBA that season in assists with 630. These numbers show that Harden is simply a loyal teammate willing to take on whatever role necessary to win games and support his teammates. **Rating: Quote Machine**

Harden played his first three NBA seasons as a member of the Oklahoma City Thunder. During his years with the

"**I took a back seat and did whatever it took for the team to win.**"

Thunder, Harden played a supporting role to stars and now fellow MVPs Russell Westbrook and Kevin Durant. He provided scoring support off the bench as the team's sixth man. His skills and ability to provide important minutes for the Thunder in his first three years helped lead the team to a Western Conference championship in 2012 and recognition by the NBA as the league's Sixth Man of the Year.

Harden's quote is an indication of his willingness to take a **subordinate** role to help his team win and succeed. Although he would eventually become a starter and team leader in Houston, his ability to take a back seat in Oklahoma City helped the Thunder become one of the formidable teams in the Western Conference and led the way to all three former teammates (Harden, Durant, and Westbrook) earning Most Valuable Player recognition. **Rating: Quote Machine**

Harden played a supporting role during his time with Oklahoma City, where teammates Kevin Durant and Russell Westbrook were featured in the offense.

"**That excitement on the court, I'm the same way off the court. I like to have fun, meet people; I like to give high-fives to the kids courtside. Just have fun. That's kind of my personality. That's how I've been.**"

Harden defends as LeBron James drives to the basket.

Harden brings an excited energy to the game, which helps his teams win and be competitive. His youthful approach to playing is a refreshing change from the serious, business-like way other players, like LeBron James and Kevin Durant, play the game. Harden likes to have fun and let his love of the game help him excel.

This quote of Harden's describes how his playful nature works well with his love for basketball. If you see him on the court after a play, he is always encouraging his teammates, giving them high-fives, and doing what it takes to keep everybody engaged and focused on one task: winning the game. **Rating: Quote Machine**

"In any situation, I'm going to be good."

Ever since age fourteen when, according to a 2003 report by Pablo S. Torre for ESPN, Harden penned a note to his mother Monja Willis, which read, *"Could u wake me up at 7:00 And could u leave me a couple of dollars P.S. Keep this paper. Imma be a star."* This attitude and faith in his ability and talent, even at a young age, led Harden to become a high school All-American, be named Pac-10 Player of the Year and a consensus first team All-American while playing for the Sun Devils of Arizona State University, and earn Sixth Man of the Year and MVP honors in the NBA. Harden has been a good basketball player at every level that he has played, and regardless of the situation, whether as a starter or bench player, he plans on continuing to be good. **Rating: Quote Machine**

Host Jimmy Kimmel and James Harden having fun during Kimmel's TV show, discussing a variety of topics including Harden's sour candy and praise from NBA star Kobe Bryant.

"I'm old-school. I'm not the fastest guy or the quickest guy."

Harden has described his style of play to be more that of the old-school guards such as Jerry West (Los Angeles Lakers), Sidney Moncrief (Milwaukee Bucks), and Kevin Johnson (Phoenix Suns), than that of a guard like Stephen Curry or Russell Westbrook. Harden is OK with being compared to past players and recognizes that his style of play won't make him the fastest or quickest player on the court. His style has actually been described by his general manager in Houston (Daryl Morey) as being "excessively ugly," lacking polish and form. However, ranking at or near the top of most shooting categories plus being considered one of the top guards in the game makes Harden's ugly look very pretty.

Rating: Quote Machine

Harden says his style of play mirrors players like three-time NBA All-Star Kevin Johnson, who was also a two-term mayor of Sacramento after he retired from the NBA.

"This year I've just been aggressive. I still have that mind-set of passing the ball and being aggressive and attacking to the basket is going to draw more attention, and that way I can find my teammates. Being in attack mode is something I try to bring into every single game, and that's what's making me be so successful."

As a Rocket, Harden has excelled in attacking the basket. In the 2017–2018, he attempted more free throws than any other player in the league.

Since becoming a starter with the Houston Rockets, Harden has been answering criticism and stepping up his game to prove that he belongs among the league's elite players. During his MVP season (2017–2018), Harden's 630 assists placed him in the top five of all players. This means that Harden was more than willing to pass the ball if doing so provided opportunities for his Rocket teammates to step in and shoulder some of the scoring burden. As an attacker, he draws a lot of attention from opposing defenses. He can create his own shot and with a league-leading 624 free throws against 727 free throw attempts, and he can be deadly on the line when fouled. **Rating: Quote Machine**

"**Being named as a finalist for the USA Basketball National Team is an unbelievable feeling and an opportunity that is truly humbling. It is an honor to be included with such talented players, and I look forward to the chance to represent my country this summer."**

Harden was named as a member of the 2012 US Men's Basketball squad in his third year with the Oklahoma City Thunder. This honor allowed Harden to participate in the 2012 Summer Olympic Games held in London, representing the United States. He played a role in the team's gold medal victory run, averaging 5.5 points a game and providing much needed relief for the talented players he alludes to in his cookie-cutter quote. **Rating: Cliché City**

"**My dream was to be in the NBA. I wasn't really focused on being a star player on a team. I just wanted to make it to the NBA. I've been blessed for the opportunities to be in the finals, been in the playoffs ever since I've been in the NBA."**

Harden left a note for his mother when he was fourteen years old, letting her know that he was going to become a player in the NBA someday. As reported by ESPN's Pablo Torre in a 2013 story, Harden's mother, Monja Willis, claimed that as a pudgy youth Harden hated to practice but carried a basketball by his

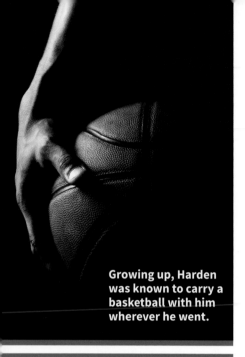

side everywhere he went: to school, to church, even to bed. Harden's mom conveys the story in a much more compelling way than her son does in this quote.

Not only has Harden fulfilled his dream of becoming an NBA player, he has risen to become one of the stars of the league. His ability to score, create shots, get other players involved in the game, and get to the free throw line have given him opportunities to play for the US national team and play in the NBA postseason following each of his first nine seasons. **Rating: Cliché City**

Growing up, Harden was known to carry a basketball with him wherever he went.

 ## VALUABLE SIXTH MAN

James Harden famously went from coming off the bench in Oklahoma City to being the team leader in Houston in a single season. He was, of course, the best bench player in the league, winning the NBA Sixth Man of the Year award in 2012. In 2018, Harden was voted the best player in the league, period, when he won the NBA Most Valuable Player award.

Only one other player in NBA history has been recognized for being both the best sixth man and the league MVP. Unlike Harden, however, Bill Walton did it the opposite way. Walton was the first overall pick out of UCLA in the 1974 NBA draft. In 1977 he led Portland to an NBA title (he was voted Finals MVP) and won the NBA MVP award in 1978. The remainder of his career was hampered by injuries, with the exception of the 1985–1986 season. That year,

Walton was traded to Boston, where he played behind superstars Robert Parish and Kevin McHale. Coming off the bench for just nineteen minutes per game, Walton played in a career-high 80 contests and won the NBA Sixth Man of the Year award as the Celtics won the championship. He was elected to the Basketball Hall of Fame in 1993. Walton and McHale are the only Sixth Man award winners to make the Hall of Fame. Harden may well be the third.

"Now, I'm back to my old ways: needing to be the leader, needing to score."

Harden started out his time in the NBA as a role player for the Oklahoma City Thunder. That was because he had to fight for playing time behind stars and future NBA Hall of Fame members Russell Westbrook and Kevin Durant. He took to this role like the professional he is, but when the chance came to step into a larger role with his move to Houston, Harden was not shy about seizing the opportunity to be the focal point of the team, as when he was in high school and college.

Rating: Quote Machine

Harden has exceeded even his own expectations with his success as an NBA superstar.

"We only get one life and I'm happy she's my mom. I wouldn't have it no other way."

Harden is the youngest of Willis's three children. She has been quoted several times about how close her relationship is to her son, who she calls "Lucky," and how she had to be both mother and father to him when Harden's father left her and her young children. He is extremely close to his mother and she is involved in every aspect of his life, from cheering him on at courtside during his games to supporting him in his community and charitable activities. Harden has even gone so far as to purchase a home for her so that he could have her nearby. **Rating: Quote Machine**

TEXT-DEPENDENT QUESTIONS

1. What former NBA star had high praise for the talent and ability of Harden?

2. Who called Harden's playing style "excessively ugly"?

3. What did fourteen-year-old Harden tell his mother would become of him?

RESEARCH PROJECT

Harden's mother is intimately involved in many aspects of his life, including his community and charity activities. She has hosted giveaways in the Houston area for single mothers as a way to connect with those who, like herself, have experienced raising children on their own. She is also a face of his nonprofit organization, 3TheHardenWay, and participates in various camps and other activities that allow her to speak about her experience raising James, his older sister, Arnique Jelks, and older brother, Akili Roberson.

Find two additional examples of professional athletes (regardless of the sport they play) who were raised by single mothers who are actively involved in community and charitable work alongside them. You may use examples from the NBA, NFL, MLB, NHL, or MLS.

WORDS TO UNDERSTAND

distinctive: Having a special quality, style, attractiveness, etc.; notable

du jour: French for "of the day"; fashionable; current

paparazzi: Freelance photographers who aggressively pursue celebrities for the purpose of taking candid photographs

CHAPTER 5

OFF THE COURT

Harden was drafted with the third overall pick in the 2009 NBA draft by the Oklahoma City Thunder, making him the first draft pick of the newly moved franchise (from Seattle). Harden was offered a four-year rookie contract worth $17,800,000, an average of $4.45 million a year. Harden played three of the four contract years with Oklahoma City, which resulted in a Western Conference Championship and NBA Finals appearance in 2012.

Failing to agree on terms for a contract extension with Oklahoma City, Harden signed a free agent deal with Houston for a reported $76.5 million over four years (the contract included the value of Harden's last year with Oklahoma City, worth $5.8 million). The contract was extended twice, first to a value of nearly $118 million through 2020, and again in 2017, based on 35 percent of the NBA salary cap of $108 million.

The new extension will keep Harden in a Rockets jersey through the 2023 season for a reported value of $228 million. The contract extension that Harden signed in 2017 was the richest in NBA history.

YEAR	TEAM	SALARY	EXTENSION
2009–2010	Oklahoma City Thunder	$4,000,000	
2010–2011	Oklahoma City Thunder	$4,300,000	
2011–2012	Oklahoma City Thunder	$3,700,000	
2012–2013	Houston Rockets	$5,800,000	
2013–2014	Houston Rockets	$13,701,250	
2014–2015	Houston Rockets	$14,728,844	
2015–2016	Houston Rockets	$15,756,438	
2016–2017	Houston Rockets	$26,540,100	
2017–2018	Houston Rockets	**$28,299,399**	
2018–2019	Houston Rockets	**$30,421,854**	
2019–2020	*Houston Rockets*	~~$32,703,493~~	**$37,800,000**
2020–2021	*Houston Rockets*		**$40,824,000**
2021–2022	*Houston Rockets*		**$43,848,000**
2022–2023	*Houston Rockets*		**$46,872,000**

THE BEARD

If you have seen him play basketball, you likely noticed one distinctive thing about Harden—his beard. It is clear to see why his nickname is "The Beard." His beard is as (if not more) popular than the player himself. Many have tried to copy both Harden's style of play as well as the beard as a sign of respect for his energy and style—that is, both his style of play and his style in general.

BEARD LIKE HARDEN

Aside from being one of the best players in the NBA, Harden is most well-known for his thick, long beard. Harden started

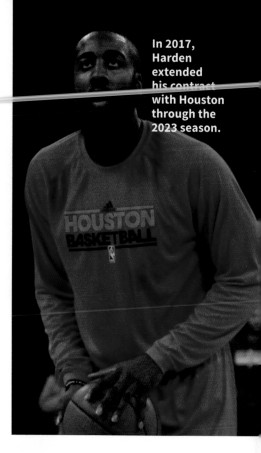

In 2017, Harden extended his contract with Houston through the 2023 season.

Harden's beard has become a celebrity in its own right. It has its own Twitter account, and the beard famously inspired a song parody in 2012 with its own YouTube video, where the singer laments his inability to grow a beard like Harden's.

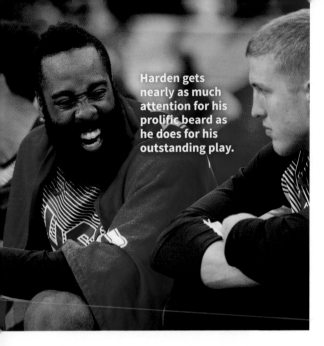

Harden gets nearly as much attention for his prolific beard as he does for his outstanding play.

growing the facial hair in college, claiming he was just too lazy to shave anymore. The beard is now his trademark, and many beard-related T-shirts have been sold at Rockets games.

JAMES HARDEN, SR.

Harden was raised in a home with a single mother and two siblings that were close to ten years or more older than him. His father was a seaman who served in the US Navy. He was present early on in his son's life, but a bout with drugs and two trips to prison saw him spend less and less time with his son.

While Harden attended Lakewood, California's Artesia High School and was beginning to improve his basketball skills under the mentorship of coach Scott Pera, James Harden, Sr., attended a handful of games. Upset with his father's absence from his life and dependency on drugs, Harden chose not to maintain a close personal relationship with him, once remarking, "What's the point of me talking to you if you're going to keep going in and out of jail?" At this point, James Harden, Sr., dropped out of his young son's life. Harden does not like to be referred to as "Jr."

Coach Pera was a strong influence on Harden's life. Since his mother, Monja Willis, worked for AT&T in Pasadena, California, an hour or so to the north of where Harden grew up in Compton, Coach Pera would often take him to a local fast-food restaurant after practice to provide him with dinner as he waited to be picked up by his mother (thus keeping him free from the influences of the tough Compton streets).

Harden's estranged father, a veteran of the United States Navy, has battled legal troubles since leaving the service and is not a part of Harden's life.

The efforts of Harden's mother and coach, as well as the strong bond Harden has with his siblings, have kept him grounded and focused. This was evident by his polite, respectful manner, as noted by Coach Pera. He received the guidance he needed to become the person he is today, despite the absence of his father in his life.

GIVING BACK TO THE COMMUNITY

Harden grew up in the rough Compton area of Los Angeles. He, along with his brother, Akili, used sports as a way to escape the mean streets of Compton. His brother used his talents at football to play at the college (at Kansas University) and the Indoor Pro League (Staten Island, New York) levels. Harden used his love for the game of basketball to play at the highest levels in high school, college, and the NBA.

Given his background and how he was raised as the youngest child of a single mother, Harden was inspired to use his fame and celebrity to start his own charity, 3TheHardenWay.

The charity was created to help provide higher-learning opportunities for the future leaders of the nation, namely children. The prime focus of the organization is helping to provide academic and financial support to kids in the Houston metropolitan area who are high achievers. The charity particularly looks for those students who demonstrate leadership within their communities, especially those facing some form of economic hardship. Support includes scholarships, exposure to college recruiters, and other assistance aimed at making the path to college more accessible. Additionally, Harden has returned to his former middle school in Los Angeles and provided financial support to improve the athletic facilities as part of his mission to give back to the community and support the places that helped him become the success that he has been in the NBA

MARKETING JAMES HARDEN

Harden's current agent, Diana Day, formerly worked as his marketing and public relations person when he was represented by Rob Pelinka, an agent and CEO at The Landmark Sports Agency, LLC. Pelinka represented Harden, along with Kobe Bryant, Carlos Boozer, Derrick Williams, and Kevin Durant at

German sports apparel maker adidas is one of several companies with which Harden has sponsorship or marketing agreements.

one time. A former member of the University of Michigan Wolverines Fab Five Final Four teams of the early 1990s, Pelinka accepted a job in 2017 with the Los Angeles Lakers as their GM.

Day took over as Harden's agent and has secured sponsorship and marketing arrangements with companies including the following:

- 2K Games
- adidas
- BBVA

- Body Armor
- Foot Locker
- KT Tape

- New Era
- Panini
- Taco Bell

Harden completed a commitment with Nike to sign a thirteen-year, $200 million deal to promote shoes and apparel for rival adidas. The deal created a signature shoe for Harden, the James Harden MVP Collection from adidas. The $200 million deal (an average of $15.38 million annually) is a nice supplement to his six-year, $228 million contract extension through 2023, a yearly average of $38 million.

KEEPING UP WITH ONE OF THE KARDASHIANS

Harden, in 2015, began a public relationship with Kardashian sister Khloe, famous for her role in the reality television show, *Keeping Up with the Kardashians*. Harden's relationship with Khloe Kardashian began on the heels of her very public divorce proceeding against husband and former Los Angeles Laker forward Lamar Odom. The two were the couple **du jour** at the time and exposed Harden to a more open and public life than he was used to.

During the time Harden was dating Khloe Kardashian, she withdrew her divorce to spend time caring for her husband after he became ill in the fall of 2015. This created some tension in her relationship with Harden. Harden, in a *Sports Illustrated* interview, described the relationship as difficult and his time dating Khloe Kardashian in 2015 as the "worst year of his life." The attention of **paparazzi** and the press was a distraction to what he was looking to accomplish on the NBA court. The couple split in early February 2016. Kardashian and Odom finalized their divorce in December 2016.

Harden disliked the spotlight that came with his relationship with high-profile TV personality Khloe Kardashian.

1. What member of a famous reality television family did James Harden date in 2015?

2. What is the name of his charitable foundation? What is its mission/purpose?

3. Which company did he sign a $200 million shoe and apparel deal with?

RESEARCH PROJECT

James Harden left Arizona State University (ASU) in his sophomore year to pursue his dream of playing in the NBA. Although he has not indicated an interest in returning to ASU to complete his degree, he has come to understand and appreciate the value of education and the opportunity college gave him to realize his goal of becoming an NBA player.

He is not the first athlete to leave school early and enter the NBA draft. What other examples (at least three) can you find of NBA MVPs who left college early to play in the NBA and who have either gone back to complete their degree or who provide financial support for education?

assist: a pass that directly leads to a teammate making a basket.

blocked shot: when a defensive player stops a shot at the basket by hitting the ball away.

center: a player whose main job is to score near the basket and win offensive and defensive rebounds. Centers are usually the tallest players on the court, and the best are able to move with speed and agility.

double dribble: when a player dribbles the ball with two hands or stops dribbling and starts again. The opposing team gets the ball.

field goal: a successful shot worth 2 points—3 points if shot from behind the three-point line.

foul: called by the officials for breaking a rule: reaching in, blocking, charging, and over the back, for example. If a player commits six fouls during the game, he fouls out and must leave play. If an offensive player is fouled while shooting, he usually gets two foul shots (one shot if the player's basket counted or three if he was fouled beyond the three-point line).

foul shot: a "free throw," an uncontested shot taken from the foul line (15 feet [4.6 m]) from the basket.

goaltending: when a defensive player touches the ball after it has reached its highest point on the way to the basket. The team on offense gets the points they would have received from the basket. Goaltending is also called on any player, on offense or defense, who slaps the backboard or touches the ball directly above the basket.

jump ball: when an official puts the ball into play by tossing it in the air. Two opposing players try to tip it to their own teammate.

man-to-man defense: when each defensive player guards a single offensive player.

officials: those who monitor the action and call fouls. In the NBA there are three for each game.

point guard: the player who handles the ball most on offense. He brings the ball up the court and tries to create scoring opportunities through passing. Good point guards are quick, good passers, and can see the court well.

power forward: a player whose main jobs are to score from close to the basket and win offensive and defensive rebounds. Good power forwards are tall and strong.

rebound: when a player gains possession of the ball after a missed shot.

roster: the players on a team. NBA teams have 12-player rosters.

shooting guard: a player whose main job is to score using jump shots and drives to the basket. Good shooting guards are usually taller than point guards but still quick.

shot clock: a 24-second clock that starts counting down when a team gets the ball. The clock restarts whenever the ball changes possession. If the offense does not shoot the ball in time, it turns the ball over to the other team.

small forward: a player whose main job is to score from inside or outside. Good small forwards are taller than point or shooting guards and have speed and agility.

steal: when a defender takes the ball from an opposing player.

technical foul: called by the official for misconduct or a procedural violation. The team that does not commit the foul gets possession of the ball and a free throw.

three-point play: a two-point field goal combined with a successful free throw. This happens when an offensive player makes a basket but is fouled in the process.

three-point shot: a field goal made from behind the three-point line.

traveling: when a player moves, taking three steps or more, without dribbling, also called "walking." The opposing team gets the ball.

turnover: when the offensive team loses the ball: passing the ball out of bounds, traveling, or double dribbling, for example.

zone defense: when each defensive player guards within a specific area of the court. Common zones include 2-1-2, 1-3-1, or 2-3. Zone defense has only recently been allowed in the NBA.

FURTHER READING

Mattern, Joanne. *James Harden*. Newark, NJ: Mitchell Lane Publishers, Incorporated, 2017.

McKay, Andrew. *James Harden: The Inspirational Story behind One of Basketball's Greatest Shooting Guards*. Morrisville, NJ: Lulu Press, Inc., 2016.

Redban, Bill. *James Harden: The Inspirational Story of Basketball Superstar James Harden*. North Charleston, SC: CreateSpace Independent Publishing Platform, 2014.

Scheff, Matt. *James Harden: Basketball Star.* Mendota Heights, MN: North Star Editions, 2018.

Trusdell, Brian. *Basketball's Greatest Stars: James Harden*. Edina, MN: Abdo Publishing (SportsZone), 2016.

INTERNET RESOURCES

https://www.3thehardenway.com/
This website is home to Harden's personal foundation 3TheHardenWay Inc., a 501(c)3 founded to provide educational opportunities for future leaders. The foundation assists youth in the greater Houston metropolitan area bridge the economic and educational gap through financial and academic support.

https://www.basketball-reference.com/players/h/hardeja01.html
This website provides NBA statistics and information on Harden, PG/SG for the Houston Rockets.

http://www.espn.com/
This is the official website of the ESPN television network.

http://www.nba.com/
This is the official website of the National Basketball Association (NBA).

https://www.nba.com/rockets/
This is the official team website for the Houston Rockets of the Western Conference's Southwest Division.

INDEX

INDEX

INDEX

EDUCATIONAL VIDEO LINKS

Pg. 12: http://x-qr.net/1G0G

Pg. 13: http://x-qr.net/1D3z

Pg. 14: http://x-qr.net/1DJt

Pg. 15: http://x-qr.net/1Hew

Pg. 16: http://x-qr.net/1GAp

Pg. 17: http://x-qr.net/1E8J

Pg. 18: http://x-qr.net/1D3E

Pg. 19: http://x-qr.net/1DZp

Pg. 33: http://x-qr.net/1G2P

Pg. 44: http://x-qr.net/1DWh

Pg. 57: http://x-qr.net/1GdR

Pg. 67:http://x-qr.net/1EMb

PHOTO CREDITS

AUTHOR BIOGRAPHY

Donald Parker is an avid sports fan, author, and father. He enjoys watching and participating in many types of sports, including football, basketball, baseball, and golf. He enjoyed a brief career as a punter and defensive back at NCAA Division III Carroll College (now University) in Waukesha, Wisconsin, and spends much of his time now watching and writing about the sports he loves.